House of Cedars

House of Cedars
Poems

Gwladys Downes

Ekstasis Editions

Canadian Cataloguing in Publication Data

Downes, Gwladys,
     House of cedars

          Poems
          ISBN 1-896860-47-8

               1. Downes, Gwladys --Poetry.   I. Title.
          PS8507.O875B5   1999   C811'.54   C99-910351-2
          PR9199.3.D69B5   1999

© Gwladys Downes, 1999.
Cover art: Jack Shadbolt, *Into Totem*, 1982, acrylic on canvas. From the Collection of the Art Gallery of Greater Victoria, purchased by the Women's Committee Cultural Fund and Canada Council Matching Funds.
Frontispiece: Jack Shadbolt, *Portrait of Gwladys Downes*, 1939, graphite on paper. Gift of Gwladys Downes to the collection of the Art Gallery of Greater Victoria
All rights reserved.

Acknowledgments:
Some poems in this volume have appeared in the following magazines and journals: *The Malahat Review, Canadian Literature, Event, Ellipse, West Coast Review,* and *Poetry Canada*. Thanks also to Sono Nis for the reprints from *Out of the Violent Dark*.

Published in 1999 by:
Ekstasis Editions Canada Ltd.   Ekstasis Editions
Box 8474, Main Postal Outlet   Box 571
Victoria, B.C. V8W 3S1   Banff, Alberta T0L 0C0

House of Cedars has been published with the assistance of a grant from the Canada Council and the Cultural Services Branch of British Columbia.

Contents

Honey	9
Hanging Gardens	10
House of Cedars	11
The Return	12
Fantasia on Quarks	13
Japanese Garden	15
Sundial	16
A Woman of Black Mist	17
TV Interview	18
Stone Garden with Wasp	19
On the Driveway	20
On the Sundeck	21
A Fool in Winter	22
Flotsam at Rose Point	24
Nicky's Crayons	25
Soundings	27
Once Upon a Heart	29
Collage Print	30
Suite Grotesque	31
Subtext for Evensong	32
Enigma	34
Lucy's Children	35
Iceberg	36
Words for a Western Trail	37
Kissing Cousins	39
Traditional	40
Mime and Pantomime	41
L'Habitant de mes pensées	42
Script for Two Voices	44
A Short Break	46
Scripts	47

The Fishing Cat	49
Three-way Glass	50
Fortunes of War	51
Words for the New Year	53
Bird in Eclipse	54
Eaton's Arcade	55
Highway Shrine	56
A Cage for the Sun	57
Scenario for a Love to End All Loves	58
The Moon on Moving Waters	61
Pool	62
The Inuit Dolls	63
At the Terminal	64
Later	65
Last Chariot	66

*To all my friends
and in memory of my father and mother,
Gordon and Gwendoline Downes.*

Honey

A purposeful honeybee
on my high clean
wind-swept deck
is perpetually drawn
to the brilliance
of a chair's
plastic ribbons,
comes back and back,
refusing to believe
clear evidence
of her quick antenae.

I too appear
to retain my illusions

Hanging Gardens

Simplest of loves, your most subtle care
a green stalking still
in this worn sunlight
dapples my skin, web
not quite visible, plain
to the third eye—
there are neither rocks nor shallows
to break the water falling,
rainbow foam, curtain between
our hanging gardens

rooted in earth and air
they are patrolled by angel cats,
Babylonian, grave, hieratic,
and when our fugitive fingers meet, grope,
dig into long electric silk of trusting bellies
these stretch luxurious and never care
whose lids half-close in bliss
whose pulse, whose kneeling bones
find comfort here
what famine or what blind god
drives this kneading

House of Cedars

Come into the fragrance of the cedars
the pine-scented
hall of singing bones

leave your shoes at the door
and touch with an innocent hand
posts where the skulls
lie buried

there can be no music
without the deaths
the only possible question is
who will be devoured

other bones dream
in carved cedar boxes
where holes drilled in painted eyes
let them breath in their ritual sleep

I myself serve the unsleeping
master of the house, keep watch, shaping
words for the surge and crash of his music
I shall never understand.

The Return

My bargain with the goddess
did not include
your rising from the sea-bed...
o not Neptune's monster, merely the usual
miraculously restored hero last seen
mangled on the shore
roaring his way back now
to the family farm

I might have known she'd cheat
though the pact seemed proof against
great winds and the folly of waters
I would drink stone, eat silence
reflect another face in streams
the far side of despair, and she
would grant me air
with just enough of mind and shallow breath
for country walks defined
by barbed wire fences—I would be gentle
nodding to neighbours

you must be back...
someone has burned the hedges
broken the grace of sleep, and look!
around that corner
all my safely grazing sheep
lie by the headland,
calm throat savaged, slit.

Fantasia on Quarks

    i

Let us now consider quarks,
one Up, one Down, one Strange
one quick with Charm

but in my eyes, all quarks
have a certain peculiar charm
particularly
those with an Irish pronunciation;
they are obviously human
like quirks and quorums,
and one can also imagine quarks
in the Ark
except that invariably
they appear to operate
as quadruplets

    ii

I am pleased they found one
they could label
with a small heart, because
the instant before the image
hit the screen,
I knew what was coming
having just used it in a poem
as a multiple of light,
now knowing it was really a quark

iii

Quarks come in fours
and can therefore be fitted
into the mathematics of the I Ching
as well as the natural images
of that changing, changeless mirror;
evidently the bland ivories
the coloured characters of the Mah Jong set
were more important than we knew—
backed with smoothly-streaked bamboo,
the Four Winds, the Directions,
clicked into place, slid
in their matching lines,
strong but delicate junks,
berthing at harbour

iv

Rejoice, Master of quarks,
that the blind mice, the barbarians
have pierced the maze
known from the beginning
by sensitive souls—Bushmen, poets,
Persian philosophers, lovers—
perhaps they will ultimately acknowledge
what made the
what made the
who made the Bang
did one quark love another,
or a Strange quark start thinking?

Japanese Garden

What falls
on the reflective
pond, unconscious
through moving
water,
disturbing an echo of leaves,
processions of fish?
O hand be quick,
close on the dive
before the bright word
falls:
an insect
darts with invisible legs
over broken water,
moves also as shadow below
on the visible sand,
for blurred balls
enormous
walking with fish

Sundial

In my spare time
I grind bones

sometimes my breath
is the only pause
silence between porous slivers
and stone

one day
they will promote me to mirrors
I shall polish carefully
a round black window
sun's unchancy twin
and catch reflections of a tapered finger
marking only
my dark hours

A Woman of Black Mist

White-coated, curiously blond, the doctor stood in front of a pile of boulders below the hill, trees stretching behind him in all directions. The end of the week. I waited on a bench with another woman close beside me, anonymous, unformed, made of black mist.

"What do you think of the reality behind me?" asked the doctor, looking straight at me. "There are two of us here," I replied, "although I do not know this dark figure." "Tell me honestly," he said, ignoring her, and my words.

"Well," I countered firmly, sending the ball back into his court with a most satisfactory ping, "it seems to me exactly the same on both sides."

The right answer. "Good," he remarked, "now we can do the brain scan on Monday."

But I still do not know the woman, nor what the two sides of reality are.

TV Interview

But what does it feel like, writing poetry?
Like many things.

*Like what? Our viewers would appreciate an
everyday example.*
Like chopping onions.

I wasn't expecting that.
Show the sharpest knife you have to an onion
peel off the layers of outer skin
down to translucent flesh
and then, precisely as you can
carve it to bits until
all the bright edges blur
liquid and stinging
as you stumble out to the garden
with fogged glasses, useless blade

Have you anything to add?
Poetry is also like twisting Rubik's cube
and the violent inclinations of love

Stone Garden with Wasp

The landscape around has already
composed itself: to shift a cloud,
a roof diagonal, distort a tree
or change from East to West the delicate
angles of hills
would violate a truth, deny a posed
part of the whole,
and so, all.

Buddha lies among the mountains
in a position of rest
and these spare rocks, a stone calligraphy
elegantly disposed in a dry place
seem balanced too, but yet
unnatural—surely an invisible someone
wielding his bamboo rake
fans out the pebbled ground.

Who would have expected the red pool,
sulphurous,
fuming at the lip of the garden
or a tiny, black-striped killer
waiting in pungent mist?

Kyoto, October 1984

On the Driveway

at this season, to lie face upward, fall
into dazzle, sun,
is a nonsense—witness
my black glasses, profile averted,
almost another face.

yet somehow heavy light
pierces the skin, changes on inner lids
to vague coronas (short-lived,
fading against the darkness)
while trees and river systems
outlined in luminous scarlet
rise from the pulse that beats
behind my eyes

idle to flinch from glare, the glancing
hand of the sun
for the moment has already been fixed
and I am here on schedule, punctual as always
for the angelic appointment—gambling
in a witless throw, dicing in Samarra.

On the Sundeck

this swollen sac was once
my left hand
the wasp and I invisible
surprise to each other
yet the hurt from a desperate
wind-spun thing, caught on a blowing skirt
carries no blame

you too...not quite...
what was surprise
was the untold comfort
of the exchange, mature sweetness
like an Anjou pear or a perfectly
ripened apple—the rest
delayed pain, slow poison

curiously, my right hand
continues to function, and my heart too
which lurched to a stop
but now moves strangely in a new accord,
healing itself, rebuilding cells,
almost restoring shape
round the bones of my bitten hand

The Fool in Winter

jealous of air, feathering silky
swirls on your window
brittle with frost

jealous of the wheel you finger
and the stylus
that cuts your hieroglyphs

jealous of the tulip tree's shadow
guarding the courtyard
of your graves

jealous of a woman you loved
and a man who loved you
above all jealous

of the masked black dancer circling,
sashaying by, who hung your only heart
from her wrist with diamonds

in this theatre of the absurd, remember—
faced with your face, ancestral,
one player cried a name and cursed his bones.

A Touch of Incest

What are you doing fully dressed
in that bed, little Marie,
with a man who looks like your father?
at my knocking he moves out speechless,
annoyed, sidles through door and dream

raccoons wake me from the woodshed,
chittering and fighting
in the false dawn.

Flotsam at Rose Point

A brave boy beareth the flukes away—
after three days
no blood is criminal in these Islands

where we offer our faces
to the glittering spite of the midday sea
our vulnerable eyes

but do not admit a distant destruction
moon arcs of madness
gashing of green boughs

admitting it we should be wholly lost
in quicksands waiting by the river's mouth
unstable dunes

no perfect shells lie angled in these stones
but we are permitted to gather agates
of a certain luminosity

our real care, searching heads down over dry salt
is to avoid the haunted eyes
beyond the sun

"We have survived"—your voice against the wind
as though the end were
breath only, bitter air

binding us to knives and whale and running boy
and brilliant fingers torn apart by light,
the strange rebirth of suns.

Nicky's Crayons

These birthday colours
are tempting—a rainbow fan—
but he still prefers the stark black strokes of conté
drawing quite simple
matchstick people

a matchstick lady
in a makeshift house
with long bird fingers
a scream for a mouth
charcoal eyelids
and spiky hair—
why's she howling?
does anyone care?

a dark man circles
on phosphorous toes
a noose on his neck
a ring in his nose
the noose has a string
which runs out of sight,
how do you tell
who's pulling it tight?

my own stick house
has tipsy walls
when one match shifts
another one falls

how can I keep
this house upright
adrift in thundering clouds of night?
a zigzag flash, a roof aflame

Nicky draws firemen for all
his mad black people

Soundings

i

Such thin membranes between the chambers of the heart, the twin hemispheres, the girl and the shaking leaves that were her hands. A shifting, organic, an osmosis. Look at your own skin. Is it inviolate? Are you sure? At this very moment someone may be crossing its iridescence, changing your secrets into myth.

ii

Images revolve, skewed dark or light by a clouded eye. Yet I saw them sharp against the sun before they moved down-wind out of range—the gap-toothed yellow dwarf, the shaman crucified, the Tartar princess riding East to the Sun of Heaven, ravaged among her silks at the frontier. There are many texts and subtexts to authenticate these splintering of bones and other splendours which you may label as you please (classical, baroque, romantic, a touch of Dali) but after the fact any eye is unreliable.

iii

There are no choices. When I fell into the hands of the living god he scooped out my skull as hive for his bees, my guts for his fiddle, my bones for his breath, leaving me a troll child hollow as a stone tunnel for the rush of his pitiless songs.

Who would suffer that harsh wind?
Who would not choose to raise by a still pond
Music and a masque of swans?

Once Upon a Heart

A chunk of sea-tossed glass,
washed clean, triangular, is quite
the wrong colour for hearts
but what fabulous emerald and cold sugar
caught in the sun
frosty with diamonds.

In the absence of rubies, it will fit neatly
these lines that bare the greening of a heart
(O bless George Herbert's soul)
but better be honest — can you face
the brutal silence of the telephone, phantom
letters lost in the mail, meetings by chance only
after the daimon's crossing?

A counterfeit gem, lighter in the hand
than pebbles or darkest granite,
it reminds me of the jellied Turkish Delight
we used to eat on the rocks
after a swim, and his teasing
"Why do I, my poppet,
always seem to be offering you food?"

A wave-corroded heart, I suppose,
feels better than none, though care needs to be taken
it may look like sugar-sprinkled Delight
but at three in the morning rasps the tongue
often leaks tiny crimson drops
tastes salty

Collage Print
based on a collage by Pat Martin Bates*

This woman's skin has exploded into stars
all splintered topaz making
a crazy pavement
head a honeycomb
crooning its curious songs

so simple to read, you think (don't you?)
black letters of the poem
slanted over her heart—but oh
the cunning of gold wire
precise placement of, cool statement of
grommets allowing light to pierce through lines
words chosen and pressed, layered
in hidden folds
a paper skin, a paper limned
a delicate embossing

why is she surging forward
like a weighted doll, on ground
that offers no quiet mercy
movement of air or stream?

your hands have stamped her veins
to golden darkness, tangled our eyes
forever in her pain.

*In memoriam Nishi Junko, Japanese poet, a presumed suicide.

Suite Grotesque

Once upon a solstice, questing
for wild roots, I fell instead
hard into a bear-trap
and when they raised me screaming
long slivers of bone lay white
ungathered under leaves

Forgot my lameness, held out my hands
to a nighted traveller in a ditch,
losing thumbs, fingers and all
before the phosphorescent lips
bubbling green froth
closed over again

The simple chic of the steel
and gold wire baskets
clamped to my wrists
is indisputable,
but Lord, for how long must I bear
these elegant stumps?

My arms still make phantom gestures, haunted,
trying to feed small birds.

Subtext for Evensong

so the hard game ends on sands
where it all began?
unlike ourselves a basking garter snake
draws some last warmth from rocks
bedded in pathways falling
zigzag to sea

                        ironies prickle in the blood
as already the night wind rising
walks over our skins and light,
low-angled at this hour,
coldly destroys our faces
slants them into caricatures (mouths gaping, slits for eyes)
of these our later selves
who are not beautiful

                about me all is dark
I have no guide—where has she gone
watcher hidden in the garden
seer and sybil
who once marked pulses
of a heart surprised that looked
for no surprises, caught
a flicker of red wings, blue-violet
crocuses growing in my astonished eyes?
when we cross in dreams, she walks
a silent stranger

                          under the arbutus roots the snake
winds home, rustling dead leaves,
but we—uncomforted, uncomforting,
beggars still with perilous stuff in our hearts
how can we in our nakedness
find rest in any thin charade
of peace or pardon?

Enigma

Angel or bat or bell?
difficult against
the golden dust of summer hills
to spell
a dark from falling into the sun...
a feathered bell
being out of nature
is this beast, air-borne
or angel?

light-riddled ambiguity
sweep of darker bone
a whole world turns
on the simple swerve of head
falling to sun
angle of wings.

Lucy's Children

I have a passion for bones
this frame which holds suspended
all our mad trappings, puts out every hour
such subtle flags to celebrate
the fact and feast of being.

And so my eye, a raging slave to form,
pierces the palimpsest, finds
through indelible subtexts every ghost
that lies in knee or cheekbone,
shoulder's slouch that marks our human walk
from Lucy's feet to here,
from here to where—black holes?
lemurs were us, but so far back
you cannot blame them for his bulging eyes
her quickened leap from sofa to the door.

curious how it crumbles
this brief bag of bones, shrinks down,
reveals complexities—lost Blackfoot hunter, Chinese pirate
that Ashanti slave—mirrors with fine exactitude
secrets of lineage, truth as our bodies age.

Iceberg

What can you know, night watch, readers,
seamen with sapphire eyes?
these poems are icebergs, thrown
from a hard and Arctic birth, flashing
down open waters

caught in the mazy currents of the mind
they dip, blue crystal flawed by gravel,
each long compacted mass
a map of snows, marking the storms
or sudden springs, or drought,
blizzards and old disasters

the danger lurks below
on this journey south—
weight, structure, subtext—
all that slow dissolving bulk you never see
as sea-lions safely graze among its caves
and dolphins melt in death

you too, if a jagged tower
rams your keel.

Words for a Western Trail

You were dead right, pardner,
you got my number...
it was fear, my starry hunter
it was fear
and your startled, slanted eye
caught it as it came
with the flame
clawing the edges of the unhealed heart,
thin skin, bruised bone

And then? After the silence?
I guess we know the what
if not the why,
impatient angels plugged the circuits in
taking a calculated cosmic risk
that the truly stupendous display
of forked lightning over the trail
would disturb none but ourselves
and a few upland hawks...
they were right
no minds but ours were blown.

or perhaps not quite so dramatic:
someone, ink-brush in hand
emerged from a black hole between stars
and simply went back quietly
though a little late
to the unfinished character
he was drafting in a continuous
translation from darkness,
we were changed
into a precisely delineated hexagram
for the contemplation
of his inner eye

You sure were dead on target,
pardner, my starry hunter
(words break and structure buckle
under the strain)
you felt the wind of fear
I dared not know
you could not see
the drowned girl in my brain.

Kissing Cousins

We played as small fat frogs
and you a leprechaun
wide smiling lips and halcyon slanted eyes
before we both shot up
thin as hearth matches or a length of string
and you became
a flying Dutchman, ball-player,
Seigfried on skates

Then one day as you lunged against the sun
the image froze, I caught
a charcoal stickman from a painted wall
spear poised for the kill
and my great-aunt's voice came back
talking about her brother
among fine china and dirty silver
"Well of course, we realized the only one
Gerald could bring back to Ireland
was the one who looked white."

Traditional

I sing you
– what do you sing me? –
my splintered self, glass
dancer upon rocks

I spell you
– what do you spell me? –
words plaited then lost in the dark
a pitted stone

I leave you
– what do you leave me? –
my rich blood clear as fresh-cut holly,
torn, prophetic eyes.

Mime and Pantomime

The people who are mine are mostly dead
they have no language
though they seem to breathe in corners,
Chinese jars, or even in my head

>their lives make hexagrams
>broken and unbroken lines
>inscribed on a curve of silence

And I in talking to the voiceless dead
may rant, accuse, cajole,
shriek idiot pleas or pardon

>they are mute,
>stay idols in light shadow
>refuse to be arraigned at my bar

But you who let me fail in murderous silence
harsh as the drifting night
deadly as snow

>loom in this private dumbshow
>like the dead
>who have no language

both criminal and judge,
accused, accuser, jury, player
on shadowy boards of roles that never change
although the morning sun divides the light
a little differently, each day, upon the floor

*L'Habitant de mes pensées**

Under my hair, skin
under my skin, skull
and in skull
delicate networks
of waiting
neurons....
someone very clever
inhabits my skull
and has thoughts
interlinear
depending
on the dependability
of the excitable
neurones
or even
the degree of resistance
on points
at the crossings

I inhabit my skull too
I live
under the intersections
waiting for
accidents
sparks
and the occasional
blowout
of the whole system
when a too-clever someone
is forgetful,
or possibly
remembers too much

even for
sophisticated
security locks
linked against
overloads
foreseen
at a million
lonely crossings.

* *Les Pas*, Paul Valéry

Script for Two Voices

She was black and squat and Lebanese her husband did the cooking
he cooks I eat she gurgled   a husband is someone to make tea with
their friendly divorce took place a year later

we get down now to real stuff she announced briskly   basics how
very significant these armless people on the Antarctic floes I mean
the ones who appeared Wednesday night breaking off ice   you said
ice you meant ice didn't you   I decided to agree with Black Horn
Rims about the ice but was puzzled over all those arms

one afternoon she sounded almost cross   you are perhaps conceal-
ing something   are you being honest with me   no anger in your
throat   no cuts no kicks no gaping swordfish dreams   by this
time   you should be producing at least some symptoms of revolt
very odd not typical   hostility is par for the course

her head loomed dark against the window's blue the folded hills
why bite the hand that flicks the switch on the vacuum cleaner
my voice was cool   why quarrel with a crutch   discard the ring of
steel round porous bones   she was not convinced in fact she scented
lies   but went on making notes while I toyed with walking on water
and the Indian rope trick

we got on really well she liked my mind   may I use you for my
evening class   zo   zo   clear   excellent daytime recall in techni-
colour yet   symbols run out faster than dead fish tipped from a
seiner's hold   you are more articulate than most   keep talking

a high red room a strange hotel red carpets curtains   crimson
velvet chairs   lightning flash outside   inside blackout
came to   holding bottom rail   brass bed   *be good o hands
be good   défense de se pencher_dehors*   windows are definitely
verboten   you have evidently been socked out of your mind into
the dreaming world

woke up had light breakfast floated onto train no legible destination
held up three days by floods outside Kapuskasing   or was it Lake of
the Woods   no one noticed I was mad I told her grandly people
don't expect it and I have nice manners

acid dripped on all my crystal loves my open hands   I had to ignore
this nonsense after all what was she feeding   her other client   before
whisking him out under my very nose by the back elevator   you
cannot have it both ways my fine feathered friend you foul manipu-
lating bitch   I know exactly what you are trying to do   how dare
you lock us up for life in lies   how can you keep us from each
other's truth   o poor Yin   poor simple-minded Yang

       then I discovered she didn't like my mother either

A Short Break
from the French of Roland Giguère

    Earth has swallowed the last fossils, and there's not a trace left of the monsters who once lived in our skins. On a flying trapeze love appears, with all its links, transforming the abyss below into a smiling valley where sleep wanders, dreamy head abandoned to darkness. Memory returns: it used to take months to bury a mask of calamity, but now, when roots are pulled up, they are quite clean—no mud at all.

    And how many days to live in this flat calm?

    The volcano turns in its lava, waiting.

Scripts

Consider me a specialist
in impossible loves with a flourishing
sideline in visions—not my choice, blame
God's secretary, cantankerous clerk who arranges
actors' appointments, ensuring
continuity of theme and scene
in this goddam everlasting soap opera

take a simple frame, clearing the ground,
the sharpest picture, honed to reality,
ColorVision yes,
brilliance of sun and moon together
then darkness that folds, unfolds
shutters the eyes

only later
when the rhythms close in, like pincers,
do you know, dream-walker drawn by a Maker's dream,
you are being written
into a script

I did not need such grief
burning out the green heart of summer,
surely my winter shelves
(ashes filter to air through porous jars)
are burdened quite enough—my cellar hoard,
my rue, my rosary, though never
hours I spent with thee dear heart, merely
the rough draft of a discarded script
laced with clichés

cover the screen,
tune out, turn off, oh please
turn off the light
I go below to break my ghostly jars
praying for my Mother and the newly dead,
don a disguise, black holes for eyes
and feather cloak to dance
this ragged weeping

The Fishing Cat

Obsessions of the waking day
Replace a twisted dream;
The fishing cat returns from ritual
murder by the stream.

All rotted peelings, peacock flesh
Torn from the bone, or whole,
Become his food who feeds upon
The vomit of the soul.

What squad-car hunts the fishing cat,
The killer by the stream
Who rides the sun down streets of brass
From nightmare into dream?

Three-way Glass

We gamble softly
on the same condemned street
dark mirror, though you never meet
my fabulous demon lover
who is here and not here; dice
throw double shadows, cards
hint of beguilement

One creak from the broken stair
and I rush to lock away icons
hide between rainbow sheets
signs of his gods,
stuff foolishly with paper towels enchanted
cracks in the wall in case the air
betray a curve, the sound-track of his voice

if you crossed at the door, his hands
would fly to fit your bones
and you would cradle them singing
to the tempered glass
of your own exquisitely delineated heart
lights in a crystal matching
angle with silver angle, line for line

look then for no unseemly
mutilations, delicate arteries
staining the exhausted dawn, merely my bones
dangling at the back of the last unclouded mirror
gambling on perfect Space or Face beyond
three flawed reflections

Fortunes of War

     i

He didn't even hesitate at the crossroads
though he caught the signs—explosions, bombs,
the time's perplexities of death and dream—
and anyhow the alimony
would have wrecked them   she was half his age
would certainly recover   look at her family!
all those promiscuous mermaids
flopping from pool to pool   but he said
he regretted the kids

a dry summer burned itself black
into a worse fall   back at the base
she got desperate   went for the old drug
a small dose naturally   she could
handle that
and straightway fell into a cellar
of laughing snakes

can anyone remember
who pulled her out to the air?
they were flying too high themselves,
dying in drumbeats, crashes
from wall to wall
but somehow she must have escaped
in an unseasonable Arctic front
because when the headlights spotted her
at the corner of Seventh and Main, the R.C.M.P. radioed
she was batting tiny snowflakes around,
still on her feet, babbling a' green fields.

ii

And the other?
oh she guessed all right   flinching
from innocent New Year kisses
couldn't complain
lady of long acres yielding nothing
but clear title
to all his heart

yet it rankled   over the seasons
ill winds blew through her branches
caring faces soured
under the masks
the last time anyone noticed her
she was standing in the wings of the new museum
embracing Felicity with such anguished thirst
you had to understand
she couldn't even wait for an hour
when they could leave the place
quietly, decently, plausibly together

Words for the New Year

"Pretty," you say—my mourning dress
its black bands lying still
on small and intricate
movements of the heart, mosaics
softly laid in coral, lemon,
creamy white and grey, a painter's abtract
textured in gouache

New Year explodes—we sing and wave,
unlatch the door to call the first foot in,
the dark stranger... I shiver, numb,
for dulling all the stars
blow darker shades,
my father, broken at Christmas,
hanging on the tree,
and the last maimed king
killed at the solstice

Bird in Eclipse

hole bored in stone
sea-anchor,
hole in lowering sky
hole in the blood that seeps
from heron's eye

am I betrayed or betraying
in this sly disaster?
   ('round earth
    eat moon
    hungry moon
    eat sun
    fly away moon man
    come back sun)
I recite smoothly the proper words
for the bird-headed Ones
who have deceived me:
the bird lies dead
someone has swallowed the sun

perhaps it was myself
whom I deceived
and I walk with stone feet
in darkness
blinded, dumb,
beneath the unmoving sky
time as a seed's husk, shrunken,
cold as the black centre
of the heron's eye

Eaton's Arcade

a quite unremarkable woman
sits drinking under a parasol
all shades of brown
she is printed in sepia
the only hint of blood a pulse
under her left ear
or is it right   images
in glass doors
are confusing as these iron chairs
curlicued hot in the sun
painted to look like bentwood

she must be a traveller
nervously touching her bag
with dry fingers I can make out
a torn cuticle   cracked nails
not too interesting really
but how curious that when I pay the bill
no one at all
darkens the shifting glass
beyond the mirror

Highway Shrine

Now that the children have all left
I can use the new improved
closed caption video set
fantastic programmes
but of course the family controls
the local station

when friends drop by to watch you
doing your act Sunday night
I remember, bearded and draped,
the saint on the Montreal Road
flashing his red neon halo at the snow
year in, year out, till finally
a long spell at thirty-five below
cracked him
not into stone, just thin marble facing
over rubble, split cement, torn tubing—
but no one ever denies
parents brought their children to be healed
that miracles happened
from my table of seven candles
I hand out coffee, murmur
bone-meal for roses, spraying for winter moth.

A Cage for the Sun
from the French of Anne Hébert

    Someone dreamed of setting a trap for the sun, so they stirred up thousands of years of untouched snow around the North Pole, shifting it as far as the horizon. They threw up a rampart of deep-blue blocks of ice, and spread out nets,
glittering with frost—a fine setting for the death of time.

    At dusk, just as the sun dipped to the horizon at the sharpest ridge of the ice-wall, it was caught and caged in the transparent prison of a glacier.

    For a long time the yellow heart could be seen beating through the ice, shooting out cold eerie beams like an evil moon in the polar dark.

    Meanwhile a whole multitude, paralyzed with cold, went on pleading with the merciless saffron sphere to roll itself straight off the map of the world.

Scenario For a Love to End All Loves
from the French of Pierre Nepveu

The long arabesque of life, statement to counter despair,
finds your mouth younger each time.

So far back the saga of quiet belongings and drowsy
conversations, the flow charts of desire.

Trees knock against these panes, cages. Nude children move
across a lost paradise, early mornings brilliant with fabulous
cars and escapades on the sly.

In a park, the middle-aged man gently savours the autumn as he
watches girls go by, swinging their hips towards the future.

Time engulfs him, and swift little dreams, electric shocks
from meeting kindred spirits, spurt all along his nerves.

Seductions nest in the blue heights, the fair unchanging
weather of the buildings, which is honey-combed with domestic
disputes, storm warnings of anguish.

This night will pass, the last will be forever.

You listen so hard, back across the hidden years (bearing
what marks of bravery and last chances) that the voice hurts the
ear.

Behind the walls, other couples sigh between yesterday and
tomorrow.

Just so does thought flare up, bodies grist to the mill,
inventing melodrama from a dance of mad fingers in your hair.

Another night, heat bares its teeth, and the long arabesque
loops back to the self time and time again, past stations of the truth.

Recycling from the depths of the soul.

This night will pass, the last will be forever.

In this pleasant film thrown on the mind's screen by a
perverse desire for certainty the sound-track goes on so long
that in the end it fades out; little flickers of the absolute
brush against the walls and our wandering dreams merge in open
eyes.

Film of an idyll, syncopated plot, characters from the wells
of memory, prompters of speeches in four dimensions, whirling
saliva.

A few stormy passages tell our story, red marks in sweat,
little deaths during fruitful nights. We are exquisite corpses,
a single cloud enough to raise us from the dead.

Or occasionally a laugh, hard words under the nylon sheets,
when birds singing in the blood have flown
from softly contoured
skin.

This night will pass, the last will be forever.

History never repeats itself, plants keep on growing in the
kitchen, old arguments turn up in new guises, and cycles of
depression become caricatures of themselves, reflections in an
endless tunnel of twisted anxieties.

Bodies overexposed to the nerves changing, to prospects of
delight. The frantic messages pile up, love's like war, you take
what comes, words and music, emotion a sure-fire thing.

Our shadows, the odour of our skin, will stay here, part
of the furnishings, fused with the wallpaper.

So life goes on, at a level deeper than surface appearances,
even mistakes have a place, and the slightest gestures,
meaningless to anyone else, are backroom deals for love,
plastering over in the same instant withdrawals and ecstatic
reunions.

You are caught up in a mystery, my dear, illuminated by
tenderness, loved till the end of time. Baring the heart is a
slow business, words mean so much hair-splitting—it's not easy,
to keep going.

The long arabesque of life, statement to counter despair,
finds our mouths younger each time.

The Moon on Moving Waters

I ran back to the city, anonymous,
flinching from eyes and the whispers
remember her on TV? she fell out of a window
some place back East.

But that crimson stain was a myth
devised in another country, and I am not dead
you lucky girl, the nurses confided
Dr. Prashid makes such perfect stitches.

Under the volcano's wind and blowing fire
the seams of the world split open, stitches failed
as scavengers clawed through the falling ash
to pillage my graves — O Lazarus my dearest brother, do you
remember the sun?

A running shadow in that lethal dark
you came spilling from your hands
white violets for my ungodly hair
herbs to unseal my eyes.

Now I follow the moon on moving waters
sifting the curious life between tides,
counting the dead.

Pool
variation on a Navajo healing chant

I am floating with my mind in the presence of the sun
    I am floating
    enclosed by a ring of palms
    a ring of cypress, a broken
    crescent of dry hills

I am circling with my mind in the presence of the sun
    I am circling
    with fishnets of dappled light
    that spiral slowly down
    waver to floor

I am seeking with my mind in the presence of the sun
    I am seeking
    to mend my fraying ties
    to the coloured earth that speaks
    with tongues of stone and water, wind and fire

Knowing death and rebirth on the evening of the eighth day
    "with my mind I walk, with my mind I walk"
    chants the emerging self
    by pollen blessed in rain beyond the Rainbow
    Blue Coyote and the Two Rising

But I, in nine whole days I have not found the Way
    and all my unlaid images swirl on the tiles,
    these waters of the dead where now
    I circle endlessly
    rising and falling among shadowy eyes.

The Inuit Dolls

My three Inuit dolls are lolling
against a dark-green platter of mottled stone
they stick out their stumpy legs
lean drunkenly together, and at night
when the Pacific Plate shivers in its bed
once too often, I rush down to find my dolls
lying flat on their bony faces.

Sinew and bones, like me... Should I
untie the knots, call upon help for a Seeing,
deal them like cards, the small torsos and heads,
look for wisdom the Tarot Way?
Shall I peer through the holes of hollow eyes
violate barriers of kindly space
that keep us human, whole?

The last time my soul's antennae reached out
into the cold mist shrouding
the Land of Singing Bones, they pulled in your image
quietly spearing narwhal to the north of the Mackenzie
my mummified heart
pinned to your hunter's prow
but I hardly need shamans to summon
shapes of your absence, or imagine the unchanging
unchangeable snow mounds of desolation.

At the Terminal

You read me, do not read me
sometimes read me so well
I am nightmare naked, imaged
in dock's black waters
flinching
in crossfires of light

I hear you and lose you
confused by shouts for this last ferry
by clatter of cars and voices
throbs from channel buoys as heart
tolling its bitter myths
swings with the tide

On this day of All Saints
day of the dead
shadow of *la morte saison*
earth and my bones
lie porous to the night
do I hear you? do you read me?

no steady bell, no luminous grace of sight

Later

If the cards call for blindness
let me remember
the ten thousand faces of God.

If all sounds fade
let my fingers catch from moving air
the cadence of your voice.

If thought's pure mirror blurs
let ravings in the dark become
the language of birds.

Last Chariot

With a charred stick
inscribe these runes
for the Lord of Singing Bones
whose eye is the double rainbow
whose laser
burned out the fires of darkness
whose trumpets swing high in the blood
to herald me home.

Printed in December 1999 by
VEILLEUX
ON DEMAND PRINTING INC.
in Longueuil, Quebec